THE TREASURY OF NEGRO SPIRITUALS

THE TREASURY OF

NEGRO
SPIRITUALS

Edited by

H. A. CHAMBERS

You can play a tune of sorts on the white keys,
and you can play a tune of sorts on the black
keys, but for harmony you must use both the
white and the black. *AGGREY*

London

BLANDFORD PRESS

First published in 1953

EDITOR'S NOTE

MUSICAL NOTATION is incapable of expressing the various nuances which negro singers employ in singing spirituals, and any attempt to imitate them is to be deprecated. The arrangements in this book have been designed to provide appropriate and attractive accompaniments within the power of an average pianist, without over embellishing the simple folk melodies.

I am grateful to Dr. Marshall Cartledge and to Dr. Will Reed for their interest and suggestions in the compilation of this book.

H. A. C.

PRINTED IN GREAT BRITAIN BY

NOVELLO AND COMPANY LIMITED LONDON W.I

CONTENTS

THE SCRAPER-BOARD ILLUSTRATIONS ARE BY ROBIN ANDERSON

FOREWORD

MUSIC mirrors the thinking and feelings of societies. Much that is greatest and richest in a nation or community is preserved through its music. Across barriers of class, race and nationality it can speak from heart to heart.

This is particularly true of the negro spiritual. These folk songs reflect the warm hearts and firm faith of the negro peoples. They are songs of aspiration and hope in the face of crisis.

It is my wish that these very gifts of faith and warmth of heart may be nourished afresh for all men, and I accordingly welcome the presentation of this new volume.

Marian Anderson

A little more faith in Jesus

Arranged by **T. M. CARTLEDGE** *(last time go to final bar)*

Slowly

All I want, all I want, all I want is a

lit-tle more faith in Je - sus.

1. When - ev - er we meet you here we say,
2. O Hal - le - lu - jah to the Lamb,
3. Shout, you chil - dren, shout, you're free,

A

lit-tle more faith in Je - sus.

Pray what's the or - der of the day?
The Lord is on the giv - ing hand,
For Christ has bought this lib - er - ty,

A

v.v. 1-3

lit-tle more faith in Je - sus.

D.S. v.4 rit.

lit-tle more faith in Je - sus.

Ain't goin' to study war no more

Arranged by H.A.C.

Balm in Gilead

Arranged by H.A.C.

Dere's a balm in Gil-e-ad To make de wound-ed whole, Dere's a balm in Gil-e-ad To heal de sin-sick soul. Some-times I feel dis-cour-aged, And think my pray'r's in vain, But den de Ho-ly Spi-rit Re-

vives my soul a - gain. Dere's a balm in Gil - e - ad To

make de wound-ed whole, Dere's a balm in Gil - e - ad To

heal de sin-sick soul. I'll take de Gos-pel trump-et, An' I'll be-gin to

blow, And if my Sa-vour helps me, I'll blow wher-e'er I go.

By an' by

Arranged by H.A.C.

Oh by— an' by, by— an' by,

I'm goin' to lay down dis hea-vy load. Oh by— an' by, by— an' by,

I'm goin' to lay down dis hea-vy load. I know my robe's goin' to

fit me well,— I'm goin' to lay down dis hea-vy load; I

cresc.

I'm goin' to lay down dis hea-vy load Gwin to take a my wings an'

cresc.

Ped. ❃

mf

cleave de air, _____ I'm goin' to lay down dis hea-vy load. Oh

cresc.

by ___ an' by, by ___ an' by I'm goin' to lay down dis hea-vy load, Oh

mp

cresc.

Ped. ❃ *Ped.* ❃

f *rall.*

by ___ an' by, by ___ an by, I'm goin' to lay down dis hea-vy load.

f

Ped. ❃ *Ped.* ❃

Deep river

Arranged by **H.A.C.**

20

De Gospel Train

Arranged by H.A.C.

With spirit

Get on board, lit-tle chil-lun, get on board, lit-tle chil-lun, Get on board, lit-tle chil-lun, dere's room for ma-ny a more. De gos-pel train's a-com-in', I hear it just at hand, I hear de car wheels mov-in', An' rum-blin' thro' the land. Get on

chil - lun, get on board, lit-tle chil-lun, Dere's room for ma-ny a more.

Didn't my Lord deliver Daniel?

Arranged by H.A.C.

Did-n't my Lord de-liv-er Dan - iel, de-liv-er Dan - iel, de-liv-er Dan - iel, Did-n't my Lord de-liv-er Dan - iel— And why not a ev-er-y man? He de-liv-er'd Dan-iel from the

why not a ev-er-y man? why not a ev-er-y man?

Fine

The wind blows east, and the wind blows west, It blows like the Judg-ment Day; And

D. S. al Fine

ev-er-y soul that nev-er pray Is glad to pray that day.

Dry bones

Arranged by **H.A.C.**

Rather quick

Dem bones, dem bones, dem dry bones, dem bones, dem bones, dem dry bones, dem bones, dem bones, dem dry bones, I hear de word of de Lord. Ez-e-kel con-nect-ed dem dry bones, Ez-e-kel con-nect-ed dem dry bones, Ez-e-kel con-nect-ed dem dry bones, I

leg bone, leg bone con-nect-ed from de an-kle bone,

an-kle bone con-nect-ed from de foot bone, foot bone con-nect-ed from de toe bone, I

Quicker

hear de word of de Lord. Dem bones, dem bones, dem dry bones, dem bones, dem bones, dem

rall.

dry bones, dem bones, dem bones, dem dry bones, I hear de word of de Lord.

Ev'rybody got to die

Arranged by H.A.C.

Solemnly   *mp*

1. Ev - 'ry-bo-dy
2. Ev - 'ry sin-ner

who am liv - ing, Ev - 'ry-bo-dy got to die. Ev - 'ry-bo-dy who am liv - ing,
who am liv - ing, Ev - 'ry sin-ner got to die. Ev - 'ry sin-ner who am liv - ing,

mp poco cresc.

Ev - 'ry-bo-dy got to die. Rich an' poor, great an' small, Got to meet in
Ev - 'ry sin-ner got to die. Young an' old,— short an' tall, Got to meet in

mp cresc.

Judg-ment Hall, Ev - 'ry-bo-dy who am liv - ing, Ev - 'ry-bo-dy got to die.
Judg-ment Hall, Ev - 'ry sin-ner who am liv - ing, Ev - 'ry sin-ner got to die.

Ev'ry time I feel de Spirit

Arranged by H.A.C.

Ev - 'ry time I_____ feel de Spi - rit mov - in' in my heart I will

pray O, ev-'ry time I _____ feel de Spi - rit mov - in' in my

heart I will pray. _____ Up-on the moun - tains _____ my Lord

Ped. ✳ *Ped.* ✳

cresc.

spoke, _____ Out of his mouth came _____ fire and smoke, _____

Ped. ✳ *Ped.* ✳

mf

An' all a - roun' me _____ look so shine, _____

Ped. ✳ *Ped.* ✳

Give me Jesus

Arranged by H.A.C.

Go down, Moses

Arranged by H.A.C.

He never said a mumbalin' word

Arranged by H.A.C.

2. They nailed Him to the tree.
3. They pierced Him in the side.
4. The blood came twinkling down.
5. He bowed His head and died.

He's jus' de same today

Arranged by H.A.C.

Moderato

1. When Mo-ses an'___ his sol-diers___ from
2. When Dan-iel, faith-ful to his God, would

E-gypt's land did flee, His en-e-mies were___ in be-hind him,___ An' in
not bow down to man, An' by God's en - e-my he was hurled In-

front of him de sea, God raised de wa - ters like a wall, An'
to de li - on's den, God locked de li - on's jaw, we read, An'

I couldn't hear nobody pray

Arranged by H.A.C.

rall.   a tempo   *mf*

Sa - viour,— O Lord!)   And I could-n't hear no-bo - dy
Je - sus!— O Lord!)

mf

Ped.   ✶   Ped.   ✶ Ped.   ✶

pray,   And I could-n't hear no-bo - dy pray;   O

Ped.   ✶   Ped.   ✶ Ped.   ✶   Ped.   ✶

cresc.   *mp*   D. S.

way down yon-der   by my-self, And I could-n't hear no-bo - dy pray.

cresc.   *mp*   *p*

I got a home in-a dat Rock

Arranged by H.A.C.

Rather quickly

I got a home in-a dat Rock, Don't you see? I got a home in-a dat Rock, Don't you see? Be - tween de earth an' sky, Thought I heard my Saviour cry, You got a home in-a dat Rock, Don't you see? Poor man Laz-'rus, poor as I, Don't you

Di-ves lived so well, When he died he went to hell, He had no home in-a dat Rock, Don't you

see? God gave No-ah de rain-bow sign, Don't you see? God gave

No-ah de rain-bow sign, Don't you see? God gave No-ah de rain-bow sign, No mo'

wa-ter, but fire next time, Bet-ter get a home in-a dat Rock, Don't you see?

I got a robe

Arranged by H.A.C.

48

To Devar Surya Sena

I want to be a Christian in my heart

Arranged by WILL REED

Quiet but not too slow

1. Lord, I want to be a Christ-ian in my heart, in my heart, Lord, I
2. Lord, I want to be more lov-ing in my heart, in my heart, Lord, I
3. O, I don't want to be like Ju-das in my heart, in my heart, O, I
4. Lord, I want to be like Je-sus in my heart, in my heart, Lord, I

CHORUS (*humming*) or PIANO

want to be a Christ-ian in my heart, In my heart, In my
want to be more lov-ing in my heart, In my heart, In my
don't want to be like Ju-das in my heart, In my heart, In my
want to be like Je-sus in my heart, In my heart, In my

(In my heart)

(rit. *last verse*)

heart, Lord, I want to be a Christ-ian in my heart.
heart, Lord, I want to be more lov-ing in my heart.
heart, O, I don't want to be like Ju-das in my heart.
heart, Lord, I want to be like Je-sus in my heart.

(In my heart)

Copyright, 1949, by The Oxford Group, 4, Hay's Mews, London, W.1.

I want to be ready

Arranged by H.A.C

just like John; {And he de-clared he'd meet me there, That I'll be there at Judg-ment Day,} Walk in Je-ru-sa-lem

just like John. I want to be rea-dy, I want to be rea-dy,

I want to be rea-dy To walk in Je-ru-sa-lem just like John.

Joshua fight de battle ob Jericho

Arrrnged by H.A.C

Josh-ua fight de bat-tle ob—

Je - ri-cho,   Je - ri-cho,   Je - ri - cho,——

Josh-ua fight de bat-tle ob— Je - ri-cho,   An' de walls come tum-blin' down.

You may talk a-bout yo' king ob   Gid-e-on,   You may talk a-bout yo' man ob

Saul; Dere's none like good ole Josh-u-a At de bat-tle ob Je-ri - cho.

Up to de walls ob Je-ri-cho He marched with spear in han'. "Go

blow dem rams' horns," Josh-ua cried, "'Cos de bat-tle am in my han'."

Den de lam' ram sheep horns 'gin to blow, Trumpets be-gin to soun',

Ped. 3 Ped. 3

*If desired the first section between the double bars may be used as a refrain at these points.

Listen to de lam's

Arranged by H.A.C.

Wan - ta go to heab'n when I die. Lis - ten to de lam's ___ all a - cry - in', ___ Lis - ten to de lam's ___ all a - cry - in', Lis - ten to de lam's ___ all a - cry - in', I wan - ta go to heab'n when I die.

Ped. ✲ Ped. ✲

Little David, play on your harp

Arranged by H.A.C.

My Lord, what a morning

Arranged by H.A.

stars be-gin to fall. My Lord, what a morn-ing, My Lord, what a

morn-ing, My Lord, what a morn-ing When de stars be-gin to fall.

v.1 fall. 2. You'll hear de sin-ner moan, To wake de na-tions un-der

ground, Look-in' to my God's right hand When de stars be-gin to fall.

My Soul is a witness for my Lord

Arranged by H.A.(

Rather quick

My Soul is a wit - ness for my Lord, my Soul is a wit - ness for my Lord. My for my Lord.

1. You read in de Bi-ble, an' you un-der - stan', Me-thu-se-lah was de old-es' man; He
2. You read in de Bi-ble, an' you un-der - stan', Sam-son was de strong-es' man;

lived nine hun-dred an' six-ty nine, ___ He died an' went to Hea-ven, Lord,
Sam-son went out at a one time, ___ An' he killed a-bout a thou-sand ob de

Ped. * Ped. *

rall. *a tempo* *mf*

li - ons for to keep, An' Dan-iel laid down an' went to sleep. Now

dim.

Dan-iel was a wit - ness__ for my Lord, Now Dan-iel was a wit - ness__

cresc.

mf *cresc.*

Ped. ✻ Ped. ✻ Ped. ✻ Ped. ✻

f

for my Lord. My Soul is a wit - ness for my Lord, my

f

rall. *a tempo*

Soul is a wit - ness for my Lord. _____

Ped. ✻

Nobody knows de trouble I see

Arranged by H.A.C.

No-bo-dy knows de trou-ble I see,

No-bo-dy knows but Je-sus; No-bo-dy knows de trou-ble I see,

Glo-ry, Hal-le-lu-jah! Some-times I'm up, some-times I'm down, O yes,

Lord! Some-times I'm al-most to the groun', O yes, Lord.

Lyrics: No-bo-dy knows de trou-ble I see, No-bo-dy knows but Je-sus;

No-bo-dy knows de trou-ble I see, Glo-ry, Hal-le-lu-jah!

Oh, wasn't that a wide river?

Arranged by H.A.

Brightly

Oh, was-n't that a wide

riv-er, riv-er of Jor-dan, Lord? Wide riv-er, There's

O Peter, go ring-a dem bells

Arranged by H.A.C

day,   I heard from heav-en to - day;   I thank God, and I thank you too;   I

heard from heav'n to - day.   O Pe - ter,   go ring-a dem bells,   Pe -ter, go—

ring-a dem bells,   Pe - ter,   go ring-a dem bells, I heard from heav'n to - day.

Roll, Jordan, roll

Arranged by **H.A.C.**

Roll, Jor-dan, roll, roll, Jor-dan, roll, I want to go to Heav-en when I die To hear Jor-dan roll. O

broth-ers
preach-ers
sin-ners
you ought to ha' been there, Yes, my Lord, A

sit-tin' in the King-dom To hear Jor-dan roll. Roll, Jor-dan,

roll,   Roll,   Jor-dan,   roll,   I   want   to   go   to

Heav-en when I die   To   hear   Jor-dan   roll.   O   roll.

Sinner, please don't let dis harvest pass

Arranged by H.A.C.

Sin-ner, please   don't

let dis har-vest   pass,＿＿＿＿＿   Sin-ner, please   don't   let dis har-vest

Somebody's knocking at your door

Arranged by H.A.C.

Standin' in de need of prayer

Arranged by H.A.C.

me, O Lord, Stand-in' in de need of prayer, It's

me, it's me, O Lord, Stand-in' in de need of prayer.

1. Not my bro-ther, nor my sis-ter,
2. Not the preach-er, nor the dea-con,
} but it's me, O Lord,

Steal away

Arranged by H.A.C.

trum-pet sounds with-in-a my soul: I ain't got long to stay here.

Steal a-way, steal a-way, steal a-way to Je-sus! Steal a-way,

steal a-way home, I ain't got long to stay here.

Swing low, sweet chariot

Arranged by H.A.C.

Rather slowly

Swing low, sweet char - i - ot,—
Com-in' for to car-ry me home; Swing low, sweet char - i - ot,—
Com-in' for to car-ry me home. I looked o - ver Jor - dan, and

To Marian Anderson

The Lord's Prayer

Tune taken down by OLIVE PATTISON
Arranged by WILL REED

Our Fa-ther, which art in Hea-ven, Hal-low-èd a-be Thy name; Thy King-dom come, Thy will be done, Hal-low-èd a-be Thy name; On the earth as it is in Hea-ven, Hal-low-èd a-be Thy name; Give us this day our dai-ly bread, Hal-low-èd a-be Thy name; And for-give us all our tres-pass-es,

Arrangement copyright, 1953, by Will Reed

Hal-low-èd a-be Thy name; For ev-er, for ev-er, for ev-er and ev-er,—

Hal-low-èd a-be Thy name. A-men, A-men, A-men, A-men,

ff

Hal-low-èd a-be Thy name; A-men, A-men, A-men, A-men,

poco rit.

Hal-low-èd a-be Thy name.

ff

Were you there?

Arranged by H.A.C.

Slowly, with deep expression

p

1. Were you there when they cru-ci-fied my Lord?_____ Were you there when they cru-ci-fied my Lord?_____ Oh!_____ Some-times it caus-es me to trem-ble, trem-ble, trem-ble, Were you there when they cru-ci-fied my Lord?_____

88

Be still and listen

Male Quartet and Piano*

Words and music by PAUL HOGUE (1941)

Some-times I feel so lone-ly, Some-times I feel so blue,— Some-times my heart's near break-in', Oh Lord, what shall I do?— Now I woke up dis

* The accompaniment need not be used except when the song is sung as a solo

morn-in', I hate to face duh day,___ An' den I ope'd the Ho-ly Book, An'

dis is what he say,___ Be still and lis-ten,___ Be still and lis-ten,___

Be still and lis-ten ___ Till duh still small voice comes through.

Duh Good Book says duh se-cret's To share my bro-ther's fears,— When I help bear my

bro-ther's load My own woe dis-ap-pears.— I be still ev-'ry morn-ing, I

lis-ten all duh day,— An' when I hear dat still small voice— 'Tsim-

port-ant to o - bey.___ Be still and lis-ten,_____ Be still and lis-ten,___

Be still and lis-ten,_____ Till duh still small voice comes through.

I've a vis - ion for duh fu - ture, A heav'n on earth I see,—

Ped.   *   Ped. simile

When all folks live the list-'ning way— A hea-ven it will be.

Slower *pp*

Be still and lis-ten,———— Be still and lis-ten,————

Be still and lis-ten,————

Very slow *ppp*

Till duh still small voice comes through.

Ped.

Ol' man Devil gotta go some

Words by CECIL BROADHURST

Music by RICHARD M. HADDEN (1952)

96

Moderately fast, very rhythmical

Ol' Man Dev-il got-ta go some, Got-ta go some, Got-ta go some, go some,

Ol' Man Dev-il got-ta go some, If he's ev-er gon-na catch up to me!

Ol' Man Dev-il got-ta go some, Got-ta

Restitution

Arranged for Male Quartet
by **DWIGHT BOILEAU**

Words and music by **PAUL HOGUE** (1946)

* The accompaniment need not be used except when the song is sung as a solo

Ba-by-lon-ish robe an' gold he stole an' he hid, Not think-ing fer a mo-ment ob de

sin dat he did.— Oh, Re-sti-tu-tion, Re - sti-tu-tion, It's a

great, great doc-trine like de Con - sti-tu-tion. If ya stole a - ny gold____ or

told a - ny lies, To git dat peace_ ya got - ta 'po - la - gize!

Den Josh - ua he got sick an' den he want - ed to die,_ 'Cause his

(Hum)

ar - my got de - feat - ed by de King of Ai,_ But de

trou - ble was with A - chan an duh loot in his tent, ___ Ol'

A - chan nev - er thought he'd ev - er have to re - pent. ___ But de

gliss.

Lawd said to Josh-ua, "If you want to be blessed, Some - bo - dy in your ar-my's gon-na

have to con-fess;   A sin-ner's dis-o-beyed de word de Lawd has told, An' in de

bot-tom of his tent he's got some stol-en gold!"   Oh,   Re - sti - tu - tion,

Re - sti-tu-tion, It's a great, great doc-trine like de   Con - sti-tu-tion. If ya

stole a - ny gold ___ or told a - ny lies, To git dat peace ya got - ta 'po - la - gize! So Josh - ua took his ar - my, clan by clan, An' he ques - tioned ev - 'ry fa - mi - ly, man by man, An' den he 'splained to A - chan 'bout de

found dat loot an' gold, an' A-chan sho did re-pent! Oh, Re - sti - tu - tion,

Re - sti - tu - tion, It's a great, great doc-trine like de Con - sti - tu - tion. If ya

stole a - ny gold or told a - ny lies, To git dat peace ya got - ta

*At this point bass runs finger across throat, with an appropriate noise, indicating Achans' fate!

mis-erb-ly de-feat-ed de ol' King of Ai!__ Oh! Re - sti-tu-tion,

Re - sti-tu-tion, It's a great, great doc-trine like de Con - sti-tu-tion. If ya

stole a-ny gold __ or told a-ny lies, To git dat peace ya got-ta 'po-la-gize.

Ride on, King Jesus!

Arranged by HALL JOHNSON

King of kings, He is Lord of lords, Je - sus Christ, de

first an' las', No man works like Him. King Je - sus rides a milk-white horse,

No man works like Him. De riv - er of Jer - din He did cross,

No man works like Him. For He is King of kings, Lord of

lords, Oh, Je-sus Christ, de first an' las', Oh!_____ King

Je-sus rides in de mid-dle o' de air, Oh!_____ He

calls de saints from eve-ry-where, Ah!_____

Ride on,_____ King_ Je-sus!_____ No man_____ can-a

hin-der me. Ride on, King Je-sus, ride on.

dim. espr.

ff

No man can-a hin-der me. He is de

pp
accented whisper

piano take over, but pp

King, He is de Lord, Ha!

mp

He is de King, He is de Lord, Ha!

mf

Roll away that stone

Words and music by RICHARD M. HADDEN (Easter, 1947)

Arranged by FRANCES ROOTS HADDEN

Roll a-way that

stone, broth-er, And let Lord Je - sus out! Oh yes, jus'

roll a-way that stone, broth-er, And let Lord Je - sus

out! They set a watch to keep Him in, Jus'
like folks do to - day, But the an - gel came with
ser - a-phim And rolled the stone a - way.
accel.
poco marcato
Slightly faster
mf
Sit up-on that stone, broth-er, Jus' like the an - gel
mf
simile

did. Oh yes, jus' sit up-on that stone, broth-er, Jus'

like the an - gel did. When John and Pe - ter

went in-side, New hopes were there con - ceived, For His

clothes were neat - ly laid a - side, And both of them be -

simile

più p

più p

rall.

The Glow Within

WILL REED (1941)

A little faster

2. The_ great, whose shin-ing la-bours Make our pul-ses throb, Were men who got a

glo-ry In their dai - ly job. The bat-tle might be go-ry And the odds un-

fair, But the men who got a glo-ry Nev-er knew des - pair. O_ Lord, give me a

glo-ry, When all else is done, If you've on-ly got a glo-ry You can still go on.

short pause

Joyful

3. For those who get a glory It is like the sun, And you can see it glow-ing Through the work they've done. O fame is trans-i - to - ry, Rich-es fade a - way But when you've got-ta glo-ry It is there to stay. O Lord, give me a glo-ry And a work-man's pride, For you've got - ta get a glo-ry Or you're dead in - side.

Trouble

Words and music by ROBERT MacGIMSEY